BEST OF
RoseRigden
WILDSIDE III

1

BEST OF ROSE RIGDEN
WILDSIDE III

Published by Footloose Enterprises Ltd
140C Woodcock Rd, RD3, Hamilton, 3283, New Zealand
'E' Mail: sales@thenaturalselection.net
Website: www.thenaturalselection.net
ISBN 978-0-473-11858-7

Copyright © Footloose Enterprises Ltd
Artist: Rose Rigden
Origination by Scan Shop

uch of our time is spent in pursuit of happiness and being the peculiar human form of life that we are, our natures take us along some strange paths and tracks in the jungles of this world. Just like a **'tug of war'**, our emotions pull us in different directions. We want to look and be 'smart'. Holding our own and yet rising above the 'herd' from time to time. Having a cause or opinion sharpens our appetites, although this can sometime lead to other consequences. As hunters for the truth or design for our lives we nearly always become victims of fad, fashion or trends.

Watch out, there is a bit of you in here somewhere.........Rose Rigden has combined the very best of her books with a sprinkling of new bait to tempt you into the laughter trap. We hope you will be well and truly 'Snared'.

ALSO BY

Rose Rigden

THE ARTIST

With the worldwide success of the WILDSIDE SERIES,
Rose Rigden's unique talent is once again
exhibited in this new publication.
From her studio in the Vumba
(land of the mist) mountains,
Rose continues to gain
recognition as a
leading Wildlife
portraitist.

 rowing up isn't easy.
All that washing, scrubbing and licking...

...and then there's the feeling of always being hungry.

7

With our tummies full,

there is nothing like an afternoon doze!

f course, we are never satisfied with our appearances and strive to look and feel better.

16

Battling to stay in shape........
whilst keeping clean and healthy.

We like to be fashionable.
Some of us go for 'extreme makeovers'.

BEFORE

*G*ompetition is tough!
We must be prepared for rejection!

We didn't see a thing all day!

31

Be prepared for drama and surprises, if you break the rules!

Rose Rigden

37

Bad decisions can be dangerous!

38

45

We are full of pride

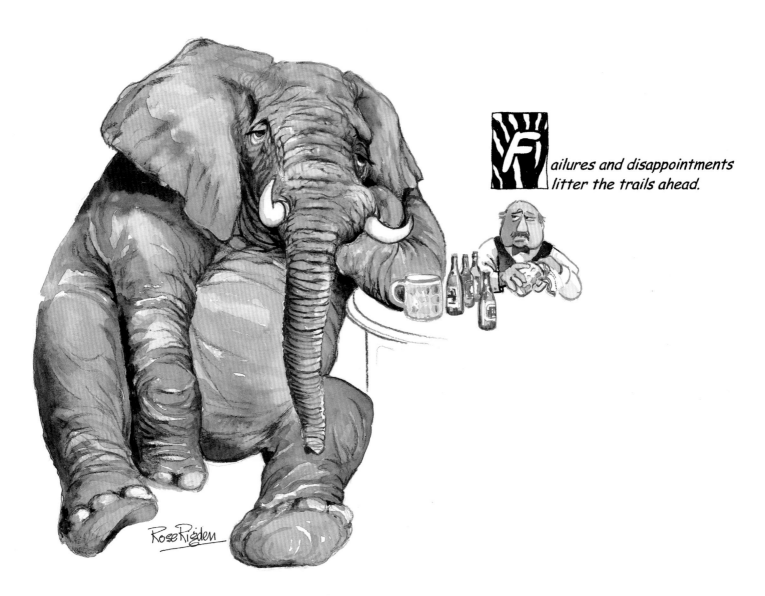

Failures and disappointments litter the trails ahead.

Rose Rigden

52

A lot of our time is spent waiting

Rose Rigden
2001

tay optimistic ...

69

Be confident in the middle of chaos!

We say things that make our hearts beat faster

Appearance is everything in high society

80

Don't be afraid to try a different approach.

Stay friends with everyone

*ife can be cruel
and the going tough!*

"That reminds me how is your mother?"

Rose Riggers 2008

So show them your WILDSIDE and remember LAUGHTER IS THE BEST MEDICINE